I0490017

Online Marketing with Organic Search Engine Optimization

By Ade Asefeso MCIPS MBA

Second Edition

ISBN-13: 978-1499656688

ISBN-10: 1499656688

Publisher: AA Global Sourcing Ltd
Website: http://www.aaglobalsourcing.com

1

Table of Contents

4

Disclaimer

This publication is designed to provide competent and reliable information regarding the subject matter covered. However, it is sold with the understanding that the author and publisher are not engaged in rendering professional advice. The authors and publishers specifically disclaim any liability that is incurred from the use or application of contents of this book.

If you purchased this book without a cover you should be aware that this book may have been stolen property and reported as "unsold and destroyed" to the publisher. In this case neither the author nor the publisher has received any payment for this "stripped book."

Dedication

This book is dedicated to the hundreds of thousands of incredible souls in the world who have weathered through the up and down of recent recession.

To my family and friends who seems to have been sent here to teach me something about who I am supposed to be. They have nurtured me, challenged me, and even opposed me…. But at every juncture has taught me!

This book is dedicated to my lovely boys, Thomas, Michael and Karl. Teaching them to manage their finance will give them the lives they deserve. They have taught me more about life, presence, and energy management than anything I have done in my life.

Chapter 1: Introduction

Too many webpage owners feel that once they submit their page to a search engine they are guaranteed success. That is generally not the case. Simply submitting your web page to a search engine is not always enough to get any hits. Most web pages require search engine optimization to become truly successful.

Search engine optimization (SEO) is the art and science of making web pages attractive to the search engines. The goal of search engine optimization is to have your website ranked in the top ten internet search hits that appear on the first page. Why is it important to be on the first page? It is important because the average internet user doesn't click on any of the sites listed on the second or third page. Out of sight, out of mind. One of our clients reported a two hundred and ten percent increase on her e-commerce sight when we redesigned her webpage for optimal search engine optimization.

You would think that the prospect of a two hundred and ten percent increase in sales would be all the incentive a webmaster would need to redesign their site. That is not always the case. There are a variety of reasons people avoid recreating their websites.

Some people believe that search engine optimization is too difficult to understand. The reality is that search engine optimization is fairly simple. All it takes is a little research and most people are ready to rock.

Other people feel that there are simply too many things to learn before they will be ready to optimize their website. Search engine optimization is just like anything else. When you first start out you know nothing. With some homework and a bit of trial and error and you will know exactly what it takes to make your webpage popular with the web crawlers.

Some people believe that search engine optimization will take up lots of their precious time. People with this particular fear should remember that old adage about time and money. If time spent optimizing your website leads to an increase in sales isn't it time well spent? Besides search engine optimization is easy, once you have the hang of it won't add much to the time you would already have to devote to updating your website.

You do not have to submit to gobs of search engines to reap the rewards of search engine optimization.

If you have a large site you shouldn't worry about spending lots of time optimizing it and running the risk of never finishing the process. If you have a large website just take things one step at a time. Focus on optimizing on page per day. Start with your most important pages and then concentrate on the irrelevant pages. By using this one page a day method you won't run the risk of sitting at your computer until your eyeballs fall out of your head.

It might take some time and some trial and error to optimize your website but you will consider it time well spent when you see an increase in the amount of traffic, the increase in traffic should lead to more sales.

Feel free to contact us via. http://www.qualitywebdesign.aaglobalsourcing.com/contact-quality-web-desig if you would like coaching on SEO or help on how to use online marketing for your offline business or search engine optimize of your existing website. Your feedback is important to me.

Chapter 2: What is Search Engine Optimization

Search Engine Optimization is a process of choosing the most appropriate targeted keyword phrases related to your site and ensuring that this ranks your site highly in search engines so that when someone searches for specific phrases it returns your site on tops. It basically involves fine tuning the content of your site along with the HTML and Meta tags and also involves appropriate link building process. The most popular search engines are Google, Yahoo, MSN Search, AOL and Ask Jeeves.

Search engines keep their methods and ranking algorithms secret, to get credit for finding the most valuable search-results and to deter spam pages from clogging those results. A search engine may use hundreds of factors while ranking the listings where the factors themselves and the weight each carries may change continually. Algorithms can differ so widely that a webpage that ranks number1 in a particular search engine could rank number 200 in another search engine.

New sites need not be 'submitted" to search engines to be listed. A simple link from a well established site will get the search engines to visit the new site and begin to spider its contents. It can take a few days to even weeks from the referring of a link from such an established site for all the main search engine spiders to commence visiting and indexing the new site.

If you are unable to research and choose keywords and work on your own search engine ranking, you may want to hire someone to work with you on these issues. Feel free to contact us via http://www.qualitywebdesign.aaglobalsourcing.com/contact-quality-web-desig if you would like coaching on SEO or help on how to use online marketing for your offline business or search engine optimize of your existing website. Your feedback is important to me.

We will look at the plan for your site and make recommendations to increase your search engine ranking and website traffic. If you wish, we will also provide ongoing consultation and reporting to monitor your website and make recommendations for editing and improvements to keep your site traffic flow and your search engine ranking high. Normally your search engine optimization experts work with your web designer to build an integrated plan right away so that all aspects of design are considered at the same time.

Chapter 3: A Brief History of Search Engine Optimization

Search engine optimization is the art and science of making web pages attractive to internet search engines. Some internet businesses consider search engine optimization to be the subset of search engine marketing.

In the middle of the 1990s webmasters and search engine content providers started optimizing websites. At the time all the webmasters had to do was provide a URL to a search engine and a web crawler would be sent from the search engine. The web crawler would extract link from the webpage and use the information to index the page by down loading the page and then storing it on the search engines server. Once the page was stored on the search engines server a second program, called an indexer, extracted additional information from the webpage, and determines the weight of specific words. When this was complete the page was ranked.

It did not take very long for people to understand the importance of being highly ranked.

In the beginning search engines used search algorithms that webmasters provided about the web pages. It did not take webmasters very long to start abusing the system requiring search engines to develop a more sophisticated form of search engine optimization. The search engines developed a system that considered several factors; domain name, text within the title, URL directories, term frequency, HTML tags, on page key word proximity, All attributes for images, on page keyword adjacency, text within NOFRAMES tags, web content development, sitemaps, and on page keyword sequence.

Google developed a new concept of evaluating internet web pages called PageRank. PageRank weighs a web page's quantity and quality based on the pages incoming links. This method of search engine optimization was so successful that Google quickly began to enjoy successful word of mouth and consistent praise.

To help discourage abuse by webmasters, several internet search engines, such as Google, Microsoft, Yahoo, and Ask.com, will not disclose the algorithms they use when ranking web pages. The signals used today in search engine optimization typically are; keywords in the title, link popularity, keywords in links pointing to the page, PageRank (Google), Keywords that appear in the visible text, links from on page to the inner pages, and placing punch line at the top of the page.

For the most part registering a webpage/website on a search engine is a simple task. All Google requires is a link from a site already indexed and the web crawlers will visit the site and begin to spider its contents. Normally a few days after registering on the search engine the main search engine spiders will begin to index the website.

Some search engines will guarantee spidering and indexing for a small fee. These search engines do not guarantee specific ranking. Webmaster's who do not want web crawlers to index certain files and directories use a standard robots.txt file. This file is located in the root directory. Occasionally a web crawler will still crawl a page even if the webmaster has indicated he does not wish the page indexed.

Chapter 4: Search Engine Optimization

When your website is ranked well in the most popular search engines, you get more visitors clicking on your site. The more visitors you get the more business you get. Did you know that about 20 percent to 80 percent of your visitors will find your web site through the search engines. Studies show that most people do not look past the fourth page of results. There was a time when you could use free submission services that would submit your website to search engines and directories. At one time, that would actually get you ranked OK. Nowadays, that won't do anything for you. You want to get ranked at LEAST on the first page of Google and Yahoo. The better option would be to get ranked in the top 3 listings of both Google and Yahoo. This is not easy.

All search engines spider or crawl the Web and automatically index your web site based on their own secretive algorithms, which are constantly changing. How do you get ranked well. You can use pay-per-click, which is where you bid for top ranking positions under keywords of your choice. Just make sure that the bids you make are not more than what each customer is worth to you in your site. For ex, if your maximum bid per click is 10.00 dollars and it takes 100 visitors to make a sale, you are probably going to lose money.

To get high ranked, you need to have a website with

fresh content and good links to other sites with high page ranking. You could have an rss feed in your site so that the content is fresh and new articles are submitted to keep the customers interested and the search engines satisfied.

Search engines are looking for fresh information, good linking, and relevance. Keep these points in mind and set forth with that high ranked site.

Chapter 5: Basic Information about Search Engine Optimization

Fifteen years ago if we need information we had to go to library. Writing reports, and preparing for test required hours of scanning shelves filled with books, blowing large chunks of change in the copy matching, checking out a mountains of books, and squinting at microfilm. The internet has chanced all of that. Now when we need to learn something all we have to do is boot up a computer and connect to the internet.

Most people have an extensive favourites list on their computers, a simple click of the mouse and they are at their favourite website. This is a handy feature if you do a lot of online shopping at a particular store or spend a lot of time at a specific chat-room. When they need to use the internet to gather information most people consult an online search engine.

A search engine is an information retrieval system designed to help locate information. Most people are familiar with Google, yahoo, and ask.com. Search engines work when a user types a keyword into the little box. Once the user types in the word the search engine scans all its files. It then provides the user with a page that is full of options, generally twenty. The user scans the list of options and then opens the one that sounds like it best suits their needs. Search engines use something called search engine optimization to determine the ranking of each web address.

Search engine optimization is the art and science of making web pages attractive to the search engines. The more a website appeals to the search engine the higher it will be ranked.

Crawler based search engines determine the relevancy of a website by following a set of guidelines called algorithms. One of the first things a crawler based search engine looks for is keywords. The more frequently a website uses a certain keyword the higher the website will rank. Search engines believe that more frequently a word appears the more relevant the website.

The location of the key words is as important as the frequency.

The first place a search engine looks for keywords is in the title. Web designers should include a keyword in their HTML title tag. Web designers should also make sure that keywords are included near the top of the page. Search engines operate under the assumption that the web designers will want to make any important information obvious right away.

Spamdexing is a term used to describe a webpage that uses a certain word hundreds of times in an attempt to propel their webpage to the top of search engines rankings. Most search engines use a variety of methods, including customer complaints, to penalize websites that use spamming methods. Very few internet search engines rely solely on keywords to determine website ranking. Many search engines also use something called "off the page" ranking criteria. Off the page ranking criteria are ranking criteria's that webmasters cannot easily influence. Two methods of off the page search engine optimization are link analysis and click through measurement.

Chapter 6: Why is Search Engine Optimization Important?

The Internet has provided ways to revolutionize how we live our daily lives. It has crawled into the different dimensions of human lives- business, communication, information dissemination, personal relationships. People have made a paradigm shift towards using the Internet to aid them in their daily activities.

With this context in mind, many people are continuously struggling to get noticed in the world of the Internet. Websites are growing like mushrooms everywhere, every time. How can one's website get past the millions of other websites and eventually be noticed by its target audience?

Search engine optimization aims to achieve the goal of getting more visitors to a website by helping it get higher rankings in the search engines. This simply means that search engine optimization's goal is to make a website appear on the first pages, if not the first page of a search done through the search engine.

There are two ways to be able to get noticed by search engines. One is through pay-per-click-advertisements. A good example of a pay-per-click system that is employed by search engines is the Google Adwords system. It has created a hype and has given Google more than 8 billion dollars in terms of revenue per year. Webmasters can place their bids to be shown when a keyword is searched by a surfer.

The highest bidders will get their sites to appear first when the search is being done.

The second way of getting high rankings from search engines is through organic searches. Search engines evaluate websites by using what they call 'spiders." These programs scan the websites and collects information about them. They then collate the information and pass it on to the search engine. This area is primarily the main arena of search engine optimization. It utilizes a set of methods to be able to get search engines to list the website on high ranks.

Traffic

The main purpose of search engine optimization is to increase the traffic generated by a website. Websites are built to be seen by Internet surfers and search engines can help it achieve this goal.

The power of the search engine should not be underestimated. It is one of the building blocks of the foundation of the Internet. A survey showed that 90% of all Internet users employ search engines to aid them in their Internet-related activities. Google, the dominant player in the search engine industry, generates 70% of all search-related Internet activity.

People and Search Engines are alike

Search engines behave like people. They like websites which contain substantive information about a certain topic. The best sites usually appear first in search engines because people like them as well as the search engines.

Search engine optimization does not only generate traffic, it helps maintain the traffic. The behaviour of the search engine is indicative to the behaviour of the people who visit the website. Search engine optimization leads to the optimization of a webpage or a website. It will lead to a website which is more organized and a website which contains substantive information.

Target Audience

The use of the search engine to be able to target one's target audience is one of the most effective Internet marketing strategies. It is not like other on-line marketing techniques (such as email marketing) which can lead to a lot of leakages in terms of targeting the right audience.

Search engines segment the market and connect the right people together. People search for topics which they are interested in and this is the main strength of search engines in connecting markets together.

Cost Effectiveness

One can do search engine optimization under the assumption that he knows what he is doing. Search engine optimization is a full-time job and has a very long learning curve. This is why most people would resort to out-sourcing the job to experts who are good at what they do. One should be cautious, however, in hiring a search engine optimization company or consultant. Factors such as pricing and service should carefully be assessed before signing a deal. If done properly, search engine optimization is a very cost effective way of getting more people to know about one's products or to know about a certain issue or event that a website is disseminating.

Feel free to contact us via. http://www.qualitywebdesign.aaglobalsourcing.com/contact-quality-web-desig if you would like coaching on SEO or help on how to use online marketing for your offline business or search engine optimize of your existing website. Your feedback is important to me.

SEO is very important for websites since it determines the position of the website in comparison with its competitors. It does not only generate traffic from the targeted audience but is also a cost-effective way of optimizing the website.

Chapter 7: The Basic Strategy to Search Engine Optimization

Internet marketers know that Search engine optimization (SEO) is very important, and determines whether you succeed in making money online or not. SEO helps to make your web site to rank high on search engine result pages, such that you get large volumes of traffic directed to your website by the search engines. The process of SEO involves choosing the best keywords for your website content. This book presents the key ways through which you can optimize your website for search engines.

1. Know all your key words and phrases and use them on your web content. This will make sure that when people are looking for keywords that relate to your niche and type these keywords on search engines, your web site come up and rank high. If your website can be found on search engines, it means that you will get a lot of traffic directed to your website.

2. When designing and building your website, make sure that your keywords are in your web page headings and sub-headings.

3. Have high quality, unique and fresh content on your website. Duplicate content can result in your website being penalized by search engines. Having fresh content means that your website will get indexed by search

engines and more people will visit your website because you have useful content on your website.

4. Submit your website to website directories. This means that your website will be visible from search engines and people will easily find it.

5. Create links with other related websites. If your web site is linked to other websites, the popularity of your website increases. Create one way links by submitting articles and participating in relevant forums and make sure that you include your website URL. Exchange links with other related websites.

6. Have a blog and blog regularly using the keywords for your niche. This will increase the ranking of your blog and website since search engines will visit your blog regularly if you add fresh content on a regular basis. These steps can help to increase your website ranking on major search engines, Follow them and see high volumes of traffic directed to your website.

Chapter 8: Search Engine Optimization and Advertising

In today's net-savvy world it has become common for any business to have a website which they use mostly for advertising their products and services. With the advent of search engines it has become even easier for the customers to search for the stuff online. For a website to be successful its link should land in the first three pages which the search engine brings and the rank of the page should be high which means many visitors come to the site. This can be achieved by applying search engine optimization or popularly known as SEO. This is a marketing strategy which increases the quality and quantity of traffic flow to a particular website via search engines.

SEO not only affects the search engine results, but also image search, video search and industry specific vertical search engines. It determines how a search algorithm functions and searches what is popular with people. When a website link is submitted to a search engine, a spider crawls through a page to gather links which lead to other pages and stores those pages on the server of the search engine. The information collected from these pages is sent to the indexer, whose job is to extract information from those pages such as the keywords and their weights, the location of the page and other links that are stored for the spider to crawl in future.

In the beginning, the search engine optimizer

algorithms were dependant on the keywords, Meta tags, and index files provided by the Webmaster. Meta tags provided information about a particular page, but using them for indexing the pages didn't prove to be successful as some Webmasters added irrelevant Meta tags to increase the number of hits and earn huge ad revenue. They even changed the HTML of the web pages to achieve a good rank for the page. But this was a case of abuse as it fetched irrelevant pages.

Search engines then began utilizing complex ranking algorithm, which were difficult for the webmasters to manipulate so as to provide web surfers with genuine results. The rank of the web page was calculated mathematically by functions using strength and quantity of the inbound links. The higher the rank of the page the more chances it had to be viewed by a person. Later algorithms were developed which considered various other on-page factors such as rank and off-page factors such as hyperlink. Since the webmasters couldn't manipulate the page rank, they began exchanging, selling and buying links, which lead to link spamming and even creation of numerous sites dedicated for this purpose.

Algorithms became more complex by every passing day and top search engines kept their algorithms a secret. As the cost of SEO increased, advertisers were roped in to pay for it, which finally resulted in high quality web pages. Although investing in SEO is very fruitful, but at the same time is risky because without any prior notice the algorithms being used are bound to change and the search engine will stop directing visitors to the page.

Many consultants are available in the market that provides SEO services. They manipulate the HTML source code of the web site like menus, shopping carts and sometimes even the content of the website to draw more traffic. Search engines like Yahoo has algorithms that extract pages not according to the page rank but according to the cost per click or set fee, that is if a advertiser desires that the page containing his ad be displayed, he is expected to pay money for it. This is a point of controversy, as only the big businesses will be able to increase the number of hits of their page but not the small business who might be having a better quality page.

Google Ad Words explores ads which have words typed in the search box by the surfer. The Million Dollar Homepage started the concept of Pixel advertising, which is a graphical kind of advertising. Depending on the pixels, the space is sold to the advertiser. Keyword advertising involves advertisers who buy URLs of a site and place their ads at that location. Thus SEO is a market in its own which is yielding great results for businesses on Internet.

Chapter 9: Pay-per-click and Search Engine Optimization – a Perfect Marriage and Popular Viral Marketing Techniques

Pay per click or search engine optimization, which one should you use? Many view PPC marketing as a colossal waste of money while others disdain search engine optimization. In reality, the two marketing strategies form a perfect marriage.

Pay-Per-Click - PPC

PPC marketing is a love it or hate platform. For the "love it" crowd, PPC marketing is a way to get instant exposure and feedback on site designs. In a matter of minutes, you can start receiving traffic and adjusting your site to convert the traffic at the best rate possible. For those in the "hate it" crowd, bids are too high and one never knows how many of the clicks are fake and worthless.

Search Engine Optimization – SEO

As with PPC, SEO marketing has its proponents and detractors. Those who love it look at the free traffic and glorious profitability of a site that converts the traffic at a decent rate. Detractors view SEO as an unnecessary waste of time since it can take a year or more to get high rankings, particularly on Google. Detractors also argue that high listings are subject to changes in the search engine ranking process, which means you can lose your rankings.

So, who is right? In truth, both sides make accurate arguments. PPC is expensive and click fraud is a monstrous problem. SEO produces free traffic, but it takes along time to get to the top and rankings are subject to the whims of search engine ranking changes. The truth, of course, is both marketing platforms should be used whenever possible.

Marketing Marriage

Every site is unique, but most should combine PPC and SEO marketing as part of an overall internet marketing strategy. When starting out, the PPC campaign is critical for getting immediate traffic and tweaking the site to maximize conversions. At the same time, a SEO campaign should be undertaken. As the site rises in search results, the PPC campaign should be phased out for the relevant high listings.

PPC and SEO marketing are not mutually exclusive. When married together as part of an overall marketing strategy, both platforms will deliver the goods. Popular Viral Marketing Techniques.

Viral Marketing is all about giving away your own free product or service along with your ad copy (contact information, link, email, etc.). In turn, recipients of your free product are allowed to pass it along to their own clients, prospects, visitors and others as a freebie. This is a quick way to multiple your marketing at no extra expense and without extra effort on your part.

Here are some popular viral marketing techniques to follow:

1. eBooks – Share your no cost eBook with your website visitors. Include a nice full-colour ad for your most popular product line with links to your website and email. Tell recipients to share copies of the eBook with their own site visitors and other contacts.

2. Software - Share a trial or "lite" version of your software with your website visitors as a freebie. Do not forget to include that ad for your most popular product line with links to your website and email. And tell recipients to share copies of the software with their own site visitors and other contacts. For help creating software, hire help from us. Feel free to contact us via. http://www.qualitywebdesign.aaglobalsourcing.com/contact-quality-web-desig Your feedback is important to me.

3. Web Host – Offer to host small business web sites on your server at no charge. In exchange, place your own banner ad at the top of the site for viral marketing. You can setup a fold for their site and they can choose their own domain name and have it redirected to that folder.

4. Templates – Design your own website or other templates, include your own marketing information on them and give them away as free downloads or as an electronic package. Grant permission for recipients to pass them along.

5. Articles – Write articles about your industry.

37

Include your website and contact information in the byline and grant permission for others to publish as long as they keep the byline intact. Then people can use your contact on websites, in ezines, newsletters and other places where once again, viral marketing will speed the spread of information about your business.

6. Discussion Board - Set up a Discussion Board on your website with your banner ad attached at the top. And invite others to link to it and use it for their own sites. In summary, by using viral marketing strategies, you can reach out all over the Internet with much less effort. See which methods work best for you and repeat them as often as needed.

Chapter 10: Blogging is your Road to Search Engine Optimization

What is the importance of blogging to search engine optimization.

Search engine optimization is the newest trend among online marketers. Today, companies have recognized that one of the most effective ways of getting free advertising on the Internet is to show up first under relevant search terms in the various engines.

Trying your best to get into the system can sometimes make your site bounce back search engines in the process. But then there are some ways of making sure that both the architecture and the content of pages is as friendly as possible to the search engine spider.

That is why web site owners are continuously conjuring up techniques for search engines to read them as one of the best. The newest addition to doing this is though blogging.

Search engines are in love with blogs.

Blogs come complete with permalinks, regular updates and with the newest and accurate content. All these in one package is enough to make spiders not want for more.

There are also blogs that spider do not like. Some

blogging habits are less useful to spiders than they could be. News oriented and political blogs have the tendency to link the phrase "read the whole thing" most often.

This is just fine for humans since they are able to see the link in the context of the post. But a spider do not have the capability to do this. Although they can read the contextual part of your blog, they do not really comprehend the "whole thing" part.

If you want your blogs attain higher search engines positioning, keep in mind that the spider is the one that determines if you are worthy of the rank.

Below are some spider-sensitive factors you have to consider when creating a post for your blog.

Use a descriptive title. Titles or headlines are given more focus by search engines. It is important that you think of a good one for your blog post. Better use highly targeted keyword phrases that will best describe the content you are writing about. Do not create one that has been used over and over again. Be creative and think of something spiders do not get to see often.

Emphasize what needs to be emphasized. Be sure to make use of the same targeted keywords that you use in the title to the content of your article. You can have repetitions of words that are important. Make them bold or use them in external links. In using your keywords, do not make it appear redundant. Use them and make sense at the same time.

Put yourself in the search engines" shoes. Search engines have clever algorithms to bring relevant results. Unfortunately, they do not have the intelligence inherent in humans. Choose your words wisely. Using shortcut or idioms is not wise. Use standard words and go directly to the point.

Look up the right keywords to use. There are many tools now that you can use to help you research on the keyword to use. This can help you select the titles and keywords that are most often searched for by your audience. Using this research can help you decide if more people will find your article on "automobiles" if you use the keyword "cars" instead.

Google, Overture and Word Tracker are just some of these. They will help you find out what keywords are most popular and the most people are searching for. By doing keyword research, you can take blogging and advertising to the next level.

Keep in mind that these things are just guidelines for you to based your blogs posts on. They are not really assurances that you will get the search engine rank that you are looking for. Also, do not be obsessed with writing just for the spider. They are not humans. What is important is that through blogging, you get to convey to the people the message you want read. They are your prime target after all.

Spiders should only just be your second purpose when you do your blogs. Just give them the fresh and keyword-content filled content that they are looking for and you will surely be on your way to optimizing your search engine position.

Chapter 11: Search Engine Optimization for Affiliate Marketers

There are no secrets on how to rank high with the major search engines because effective search engine optimizations are now immense.

Search engines are into providing their users with the most relevant and up-to-date information to match the search term that was used. They are sophisticated pieces of technology which allow users to quickly find relevant websites by searching for a word or a phrase. Search engine results are useless to users if the information does not relate to the search term, or if the results are old. People expect the most up-to-date and fresh information that is useful to them.

Updating your website everyday and adding some materials will help you get noticed by the search engines. So, if you are going to sell any type of product or service online, you have to optimize your website for the search engines, in order to boost traffic and sales. It is because over 90% of your business will likely come directly from search engine results. And for that reason, it is absolutely important to optimize your site for search engines for you to have the greatest deals in the entire world.

Search engine optimization (SEO) is the process by which webmasters or online business owners utilize strategic copy to augment their website's status. It is certain that the internet has grown so fast over the years and the competition for the best search engine position has created an enormous market. Therefore, better understanding the fundamental elements of Search Engine Optimization is vital for an online business" success.

Making use of effective search engine optimization techniques will improve the page rank of your website. There are many tricks that can be used to increase page rank; the most effective method is to provide high quality content consistently. This seems like a simple concept but there are many websites that fails to provide content that visitors find interesting. Sites which provide content that are interesting, well-written and regularly updated create highly engaged visitors who are more likely to return to the website in the coming days. So, if you can set your website apart from those boring, lifeless sites then do it. You"ll surely have a step closer to achieving high page rank through search engine optimization.

The next significant factor for an effective search engine optimization is to include keywords and phrases within your content. To make sure that you are properly targeting your market, you have to make sure that the keywords and phrases you have on your site are the keywords and phrase that your site is actually optimized for. The more keywords you use in your content, the more likely it is that online visitors will find your site when they do some research with those words. If you are unfailing with these techniques, then your overall search engine optimization will increase, boosting your page rank.

You should also have to develop a linking strategy as a part of your search engine optimization. Not only does this provide free advertising for your site, but it makes the impression that your site is imperative because of its affiliated links. For each link that you have pointing back to you, that is another chance for your potential customer to find you. The more inbound links that you have pointing to your site, the higher you will be ranked in the search engines.

Another is to develop a content stratagem. People who get to search from the internet are looking for information. The more information you provide for them and the more helpful it is, the more likely you will make the sale. Writing articles is the most effective way to build up content for your site. When writing articles to post on your site, make sure that you develop a clear means of arranging their content. You can do this by simply adding a new page to your site. This will allow room for extra articles to be added as you write them, and will allow you to build up an archive of articles which will maintain to draw online visitors. Make sure also that you have included your archived articles in a directory that is next to the root web of your site so that the search engines will catalogue your online articles.

Always keep in mind that search engine optimization methods are important in developing your site's status. With that thing in mind, make sure that you write high-quality, keyword rich content and link your site to and from a deliberate family of other sites. These things will help improve your site's popularity and coerce increased business through your online business.

Chapter 12: Making Money with Articles: Learn to use Search Engine Optimization Techniques

Learn to use search engine optimization techniques when writing your articles. If hiring a writer to write articles for you, you can choose one who already knows about SEO or you can supply them with a list of keywords and let them know where they should be placed and how many times they should be repeated throughout the article.

Optimizing your articles for search engines will help them rank higher when someone searches for a keyword relating to your subject, which means that you will receive more visitors because more people will actually see your URL. It is a fact that most visitors do not look past the first search engine result page and by the third search engine results page there is practically no audience left for you to promote to. What this means for those on the third or high page is no traffic.

This is why it is very important for you to make sure that your articles are prepared in a way that will eventually get them to that first or second search engine results page.

Feel free to contact us via.
http://www.qualitywebdesign.aaglobalsourcing.com/

contact-quality-web-desig if you would like coaching on SEO or help on how to use online marketing for your offline business or search engine optimize of your existing website. Your feedback is important to me.

Chapter 13: Search Engine Optimization Budgeting

For arguments sake let's say that you own a successful bed and breakfast in the middle of Devon. Currently you rely mainly on word of mouth and repeat customers. You cannot help wandering if creating a website won't help attract more attention to your little business.

A quick internet search has you rethinking your plans. There are a lot of bed and breakfast with web pages. You cannot help but wonder what you could possibly do to get your webpage noticed.

The key to a successful webpage is search engine optimization.

Search engine optimization is the art and science of making your website attractive to the internet's search engines. The more attractive your website is the search engines the higher they will rank your little bed and breakfast. The higher your website ranks the more people, hopefully, will check your website out.

The first step towards a successful website is getting it submitted to a search engine. Search engine submission is the act of getting your website listed with the search engines. Search engine submission can also be referred to as search engine registration.

One of the first things you want to consider is how

much you are willing to spend to submit your website to a search engine. It is possible to have your site listed for free; paying for the service will generate more traffic to your website. The cost of submitting your website to Yahoo's search engine is about three hundred dollars a year. The three hundred dollars pays for Yahoo's human compiled directory. The humans help influence web crawlers to your website. If you can't afford the three hundred dollars for the human compiled directory try to list your website and see if any of the search engine crawlers locate it. You can go back in a few months time and pay for a human compiled search engine later.

There businesses that, for a fee, can help you design a website that will attract web crawlers to your website. Many of these businesses charge different prices for different search engine optimization packages. Types of search engine optimization services some of these companies offer include naming convention, keyword density/syntax, blog implementation, vertical affiliates, and third-party posting. When looking for a business or search engine consultant looks for reciprocal links, keyword strategies, knowledge of HTML, language skills, knowledge of search engine optimization boosters, submission strategies, and submission tracking,

If you decide to use a search engine optimization company take your time and shop around. Ask questions. Avoid any companies that guarantee instant success, if it sounds too good to be true it probably is. Try to find a search engine optimization company that will work to build the targeted content of your website. Look for a company that offers interactive features that create documents that will lead web crawlers to your website.

When it comes to the cost of search engine submission and search engine optimization spending less simply means it might take a little longer to realize your goals. The more you are able to spend the faster your website will gain attention.

Feel free to contact us via. http://www.qualitywebdesign.aaglobalsourcing.com/ contact-quality-web-desig if you would like coaching on SEO or help on how to use online marketing for your offline business or search engine optimize of your existing website. Your feedback is important to me.

Chapter 14: Search Engine Optimization and why you have to use It

E-commerce is a cut throat business. You have to arm yourself with the proper know-how and the tools to make your site a cut above the rest. Each day, more and more sites are clambering to optimize their rankings in websites and if you lose your guard, you may just get trampled on and be left in the abyss filled with so many failed e-commerce sites.

Search Engine Optimization or SEO is a term widely used today by many e-commerce sites. For the past few years and the next ten years or so, search engines would be the most widely used internet tool to find the sites that they need to go to or the product or information they need.

Most people that use search engines use only the ten top search results in the first page. Making it to the first page, more so to the top three is a barometer of a sites success in search engine optimization. You will get a higher ratio of probability in being clicked on when you rank high. The more traffic for your site, the more business you rake in.

But, it is essential to grab a hold of that spot or make your ranking even better. As I aforementioned, each day is a new day for all e-commerce sites to make themselves rank higher using search engine optimization. It is imperative to make your site better and better everyday.

So just what is search engine optimization and do you have to use it? The answer to why you have to use it is an easy one. You need search engine optimization to be number one, or maybe at least make your site income generating.

With search engine optimization you can get the benefit of generating a high traffic volume. Let's just say you get only a turn out of successful sales with 10 to 20 percent of your traffic. If you get a hundred hits or more a day, you get a good turn out of sales already. If you get only twenty to ten hits a day, you only get one or two if not any at all.

So once again, what is search engine optimization? Search engine optimization is utilizing tools and methods in making your site top ranking in the results of search engines. Getting yourself in the first page and better yet in the top half of the page will ensure that your site will generate public awareness of your site's existence and subsequently generate more traffic, traffic that could lead to potential income and business.

Search engine optimization requires a lot of work to be fully realized. There are many aspects you have to change in your site or add as well to get search engine optimization. These will include getting lots of information about the keyword phrases that are popular in regards to your sites niche or theme.

You may also need to rewrite your sites contents so

that you could get the right keyword phrases in your site without making it too commercial but light and informative. There are certain rules and guidelines to be followed with making your site's content applicable and conducive to search engine optimization.

You will also need to collaborate with many other sites so that you could get link exchanges and page transfers. The more inbound and outbound traffics generated by sites among others are one of the components search engines uses to rank sites.

Try to search the internet for many useful help. Tips, guidelines and methods for search engine optimization are plenty to be found. Read many articles that can help you optimize your site in search engine results. The more knowledge and information you gather the better. This will all help you in getting those high rankings. This may require a little time and effort in your part but the benefits will be astounding.

If you can part with some money, there are many sites in the internet that can help you in search engine optimization. There are many sites that help in tracking keyword phrases that can help your site. There are also some content writers that have lots of experience in making good keyword laden content for your sites that have good quality.

Feel free to contact us via http://www.qualitywebdesign.aaglobalsourcing.com/contact-quality-web-desig if you would need help on this. Act now and see the benefits garner with search engine optimization. All of these will result to better traffic and more business for your site and company.

Chapter 15: Search Engine Optimization Simplified

Chances are good that at some point in your life you ran a search on an online search engine and instead of one hit you received pages and pages of possible hits. Have you ever wondered if the order the websites appear on search was just a random grouping or if they had been placed in a specific order that just appeared disorderly to you? The answer is that there is a very elaborate system used to determine where a website appears during an internet search. The process is something called search engine optimization.

Search engine optimization is the science and art of making web pages attractive to search engines.

Next time you run an internet search look at the bottom of the page. Chances are good that there will be a list of page numbers (normally written in blue) for you to click if you can't find exactly what you are looking for on the first page. If you actually look further than the second page you will part of a minority. Studies and research have shown that the average internet user does not look further than the second page of potential hits. As you can imagine it is very important to websites to be listed on the first two pages.

Webmasters use a variety of techniques to improve their search engine ranking.

The first thing most webmasters (or website designers) do is check their meta tags. Meta tags are special HTML tags that provide information about a web page. Search engines can easily read Meta tags but they are written with special type of text that is invisible to internet users. Search engines rely on meta tags to accurately index the web sites. Although meta tags are a critical step in search engine optimization they alone are not enough to have a web site receive top ranking.

Search engines rely on a little device called a web crawler to locate and then catalogue websites. Web crawlers are computer programs that browse the World Wide Web in a methodical, automated manner. Web crawlers are also sometimes called automatic indexers, web spiders, bots, web robots, and/or worms. Web crawlers locate and go to a website and "crawl" all over it, reading the algorithms and storing the data. Once they have collected all the information from the website they bring it back to the search engine where it is indexed. In addition to collecting information about a web site some search engines use web crawlers to harvest e-mail addresses and for maintenance tasks. Each search engine has their own individual web crawlers and each search engine has variations on how they gather information.

Most webmasters feel that proper use and placement of keywords helps catch the attention of web crawlers and improve their websites ranking. Most webmaster like to design their websites for ultimate search engine optimization immediately but there aren't any rules that say you can't go back to your website at any time and make improvements that will make it more attractive to search engines.

Chapter 16: Spamdexing the Bane of Search Engine Optimization

Methods that manipulate the relevancy or prominence of resources indexed by a search engine, usually in a manner inconsistent with the purpose of the indexing system is called Spamdexing.

The sheer amount of information available on the internet is mind-boggling. In 2000 a study indicated that the internet's search engines where only capable of indexing approximately sixteen percent of available pages. That sixteen percent adds up to pages and pages of potential hits. There are typically ten hits per page. The average internet user never goes further than the first set of ten. Webmasters use a variety of techniques to increase their ranking. The art and science of making web pages attractive to the search engines is called search engine optimization.

The importance of a high search engine ranking started driving webmasters to use a variety of tricks to improve their ranking the middle of the 1990's. On May 22, 1996 The Boston Herald printed an article written by Eric Convey titled "Porn Sneaks Way Back on Web." It is the first time the term spamdexing was used. The word spamdexing is the merging of the word spam, the internets term for unsolicited information, and indexing.

There are two types of spamdexing. The terms are

content spam and link spam.

Content spam is the use of techniques that alter the search engines view of the pages content. Some methods of content spam include the use of hidden text, keyword stuffing, Meta tag stuffing, doorway pages, and scraper sites.

Taking advantage of link-based ranking algorithms which in turn gives a higher ranking to a website is called link spam. Link spam methods include link farms, hidden links, Sybil attack, wiki spam, spam blogs (also referred to as splogs), page hijacking, buying expired domains, and referrer log spamming.

Some people consider spamdexing a black hat method of internet search engine classification.

Key word stuffing is a favorite type of content spamdexing. Key word stuffing is including a key word hundred of times on a single webpage. Given the sheer volume of the word the search engine automatically gives that particular webpage a higher ranking then one that might use the word legitimately. Most websites that employ keyword stuffing place the words at the bottom of the page or write it with text that the person surfing the web can't see. Some search engines try to discourage key word stuffing by ranking websites with an excessive number of keywords at the bottom of the ranking.

Some web masters like to include the name of a famous person on their site as a keyword. The name attracts the attention of search engines and web surfers even though the web site has nothing to do with the person.

Some websites try to steal web surfers from their competitors by including their name as a keyword in the body text and meta tags. By doing this the webmaster has guaranteed that the search engines with index it accurately. Using the name of a competitor in the body of a website is normally a direct violation of the copyright law.

Chapter 17: Search Engine Optimization and the Knight

On October 15, 1881 a baby by the name of Pelham Grenville Wodehouse (Plum to his friends) was born. In 1996, one hundred and fifteen years later, a brand new internet search engine would be named in honour of him, sort of.

P.G. Wodehouse was an extremely popular English writer who had a flair for comedy. Magazines like The Saturday Evening Post and The Strand serialized his novels while he spent time in Hollywood working as a screenwriter. P.G. Wodehouse had an incredibly prolific flair for writing. His writing career officially started in 1902 and ended in 1975. During that time he wrote ninety-six books, several collections of short stories, screenplays, and one musical.

When he was ninety-three years old, P.G. Wodehouse was made a Knight of the British Empire. Two of Mr. Wodehouse's most famous characters(or perhaps infamous, depending on your point of view), are the bumbling Bertie Wooster and his long suffering valet, Jeeves.

P.G. Wodehouse will always be remembered for his comedic approach to writing.

In 1996, when Garret Gruener and David Warthen needed a name for the internet search engine they created they choose the name of Wodehouse's fictional valet. The website was called Ask Jeeves. Jeeves remained the search engines mascot until the company retired him on February 27, 2006 a decision they announced on September 23, 2005. Jeeves retirement prompted the internet search engine to create a page titled "Where's Jeeves", that listed a variety of creative activities, including growing grapes and space exploration, the valet planned to do during his retirement. With Jeeves retired the search engine simply became Ask.com. During his reign at Ask Jeeves, the valet was always impeccably dressed in a beautifully tailored black suit, shiny shoes, and red tie. Although his posture changed almost yearly on the company logo he always had the same amicable smile.

When it was first created the idea behind Ask.com (back then it was still Ask Jeeves) questions would be posed in regular language and answers would be hunted down and provided. The creators of Ask Jeeves (now Ask.com) hoped that internet users would be drawn to the intuitive, user friendly style.

The growing popularity of keyword search engines like Yahoo! and Google prompted the powers-that-be at Ask Jeeves to overhaul their search engine to include keyword searches in addition to answering questions. Because Ask.com was not as quick to index new websites as some of its competitors it was not bogged down with computer generated linkspam, when users were unable to find usable web pages on the three most popular internet search engines, they turned to Ask.com who still had viable pages readily available.

Today, Ask.com uses the ExpertRank algorithm to provide its users with search results. Ask.com uses link popularity and subject-specific popularity to help determine rankings.

Ask.com has sold technology has been sold to additional corporations including Toshiba and Dell. A variety of web destinations, including country specific, sites such as; Germany, Italy, Excite, Japan, the United Kingdom, the Netherlands, Spain, IWon.com, Bloglines, and Ask For Kids are owned by Ask.com.

Chapter 18: Search Engine Optimization Hoaxes

Google believes in having a good time. They especially believe in having a good time on April Fools Day. How does a company who runs a search engine celebrate April Fool's Day? They set up search engine hoaxes. April Fool's Day hoaxes are fast becoming a Google tradition.

On April 1, 2000, Google announced its brand new form of search technology, a technology they cheerfully named MentalPlex. How did MentalPlex work? Brainwaves, all the searcher had to do was think about what they wanted to search for, this eliminated the need for typing, effectively eliminating the issue of spelling errors.

In 2002, Google openly discussed the genius behind its PageRank system. The secret? Pigeons or rather PigeonRank. Google was very proud of the way they had created a more efficient and cost effective way to rank pages. They were quick to explain that no pigeons were cruelly treated.

April 2004 offered Google employees the opportunity to work at the Google Lunar/Copernicus Center...on the moon. This April Fool's Day prank made several tongue-in-cheek references to WindowXP's visual style. They named the operating system Luna/X paying homage to Linux.

Google broke into the beverage industry in 2005 with their Google Gulp. People who drank Google Gulp would be able to get the most out of their Google search engines because they would be increasing their intelligence with every swallow. Google Gulp worked through a series of algorithms that used a real time analysis of the drinkers DNA and made precise adjustments to the brains neurotransmitters. Google Gulp came in a variety of flavors including Google Grape (glutamatic acid), Sero-Tonic Water (serotonin), Sugar-Free Radical (free radicals), and Beta Carroty (beta carotene).

2006 was a time for romance. Google created Google Romance. Google's catch phrase, which appeared on the main search page was, "Dating is a search problem. Solve it with Google Romance." Google users were invited to use Soul mate Search which would send them on a Contextual Date. Google invited people to "post multiple profiles with a bulk upload."

Google has also taken advantage of April Fool's Day to announce very real changes in the company. The reason they make real offers to consumers on April Fool's Day is so that the consumers will think that it's a hoax, joke about it, and then be pleasantly surprised when they find out that its real. Google announced the launch of Gmail, e-mail that was free to the consumer and provided one entire gigabyte of storage (that amount of storage for free was unheard of at the time), on March 31, 2004 (most consumers found out about it on the morning of the first). Exactly one year later they announce that they were increasing the one gigabyte of storage to two gigabytes.

Google's map of the moon was added to Google maps on July 20, 2005. The map of the moon was semi-real, it did show NASA images of a very small section of the moon, but zooming in on the tiny section presented viewers with a photograph of Swiss cheese. There was also the location of all moon landings on the map. The map was Google's way of celebrating the thirty-sixth anniversary of the first man on the moon but many consumers assumed that it was an extension on the Google Copernicus hoax. Google claims, through something called Google Moon, that in the 2069, Google Local will support all lunar businesses and addresses.

Chapter 19: Three Basic Steps to Search Engine Optimization

Search engine optimization is the art and science of making web pages appear attractive to the search engines. The better optimized a website is, the higher the ranking it will receive from a search engines web crawlers, the higher its ranking the more traffic your website will have, the more traffic your website has the more profit your website will generate. The key is good internet search engine optimization.

Why is having a receiving a high ranking so important to the future success of your online business? Studies have shown that consumers seldom look at websites that do not rank a spot on of the first two pages the search engines displays. Websites that receive a ranking that places them on the third page (or any other pages after that) see a significantly lower amount of traffic at their websites then one that is ranked on the second page. There is even a staggering difference between the first and second page. In the world of e-commerce ranking and strong search engine optimization is everything.

At first search engine optimization may feel like trying to rappel down the Grand Canyon, a huge scary world full of big words like web crawlers, PageRank, Meta tags, and algorithms. You've never heard of any of these things. A quick internet search of the world algorithm does not help; all you got was a printout of strange symbols and numbers arranged in complex algebraic equations.

Sit back, take a deep breath, and try to relax. Search engine optimization is a lot simpler than you might think. First things first.

Algorithms really are every bit as complex as they look. Simply defined they are a finite set of carefully defined instructions. Most, if not all, computer programs are designed with strict algorithms.

PageRank is simply the program Google designed to search, index, and rank it registered webpage's. PageRank operates on a link analysis algorithm. PageRank is credited for Google incredible success.

Web crawlers are tools search engines use to browse the World Wide Web in a methodical, automated manner. When web crawlers are browsing websites they are looking for algorithms.

Meta tags are special HTML tags that provide information to about a web page. Meta tags are written directly into the title tag and are only visible to the search engine.

The reality of search engine optimization is that you can start to optimize your website without any knowledge at all of the technical stuff involved in search engine optimization. Simply stated the very first step in designing a website that is going to be well ranked by the search engines is to create a content rich site. What this means is that you must cram as much information about your product into your website as you possibly can.

The third step to search engine optimization is to fill your site with keywords that will attract the web crawler's attention. The final step in a wonderfully optimized website is to submit it to the search engine that will compliment it.

Chapter 20: Yahoo Search Engine Optimization

Jerry Yang and David Filo were graduate students at Stanford University in January of 1994 when they created a website that they called "Jerry's Guide to the World Wide Web," a directory that organized other web sites into a hierarchy. Four months later Yang and Filo renamed the search engine Yahoo! after a word used by Jonathan Swift in Gulliver's Travels. Swift's definition of Yahoo! was "rude, unsophisticated, uncouth."

At the end of 1994, approximately twelve months after its creation, Yang and Filo had over one million hits on their fledgling search engine. Understanding that they had designed something that could enjoy potential business success Filo and Yang incorporated Yahoo! early in March of 1995, fourteen months after its inception. Because the name Yahoo was already the brand name of other enterprises, human propelled watercraft, barbecue sauce, and knives, Yang and Filo were forced to add the exclamation point in order to trademark the name. Yahoo! had it first public offering on April 12, 1996. Two point six million shares of Yahoo! were sold at thirteen dollars a piece, earning a total of thirty-three point eight million dollars.

By the late 1990's Yahoo! and several other internet communications company's diversified into web portals.

In the late 1990's Yahoo! also started buying out other companies such as eGroups and GeoCities. Because Yahoo! had a reputation for changing terms of service when purchasing companies most of the buy outs were wrought with controversy.

Although it stocks fell to an all time low, Yahoo! was able to survive the dot.com bubble burst. In order to help rebuild itself, Yahoo! started forming partnerships with telecommunication companies and internet providers, these alliances led to the creation of content rich broadband services that actively competed with AOL.

With their eye on the future, the powers in charge at Yahoo! are working on creating Yahoo!Next, a concept similar to Google Labs that contains forums that provide places for Yahoo! users to leave feedback that will hopefully assist in the development of future Yahoo! enterprises and technologies.

Like most successful companies Yahoo! is constantly working to improve and expand. Yahoo! currently provides its customers with a smorgasbord of internet services that cater for most online activities. These services include Yahoo! Mail, Yahoo! Groups, Yahoo! Maps and Driving Directions, and Yahoo! Messenger. While Google holds the top spot in search engines Yahoo! is standing strong in second place. Yahoo! competes against Yahoo! by offering its customers vertical search services such as, Yahoo! Image, Yahoo! Local, Yahoo! Shopping Search, Yahoo! Video, and Yahoo! News. Yahoo! is proud to boast the largest, most successful e-mail service in the world.

User generated content products such as Yahoo! Personals, Yahoo! Photos, Yahoo! 360, and Flicker offer Yahoo!'s customer's social networking services.

Yahoo! Shopping, Yahoo! Merchant Solutions, Yahoo! Store, Yahoo! Web Hosting, Yahoo! Domains, and Yahoo! Business Email are services Yahoo! provides to small business owners that allows them to develop their own online business using Yahoo!'s tools.

In March of 2004 Yahoo! launched a paid inclusion program that guaranteed commercial websites listings on Yahoo! search engines for a fee. While the paid inclusions were lucrative for Yahoo!, they where unpopular with the online marketing world. Business owners did not want to pay the internet mogul for search engine optimization. Paid inclusion simply guaranteed that the businesses websites would be ranked; it did not guarantee that it would be ranked in the first two pages.

Chapter 21: Natural Search Engine Optimization or Pay-per-click

The internet is literally like having the world at ones fingertips. Not only does it provide families a cheap way to stay in touch (e-mail and instant messaging), it allows students to cram for finals and write last minute papers in the middle of the night, long after the library has closed, but the internet is suddenly a way for the smallest business to break into a global market.

Let's pretend that you are the owner of a small novelty store in a small rural town in the Scotland. Most of your merchandise is handmade trinkets and crafts created by the residents of the small town (on commission so the up front cost of most of your merchandise is minimal). Although business is slow during the winter months during the tourist season you turn a tidy profit. One day as a Chicago tourist purchases a photo of the late afternoon sun glinting off a herd of sleeping cattle she mentions that she wishes you had a website so she could purchase quaint Christmas gifts for her family. As she leaves the story, her wrapped photograph tucked under her arm, you stare at your computer.

The internet could be a cheap way to increase your profit margin. You already have your physical business; a website would simply be an addition. You look at all the pretty knickknacks arranged throughout the store. If you expanded your business to include a website you could sell Scottish trinkets all over the world. It wouldn't take that much time. You have a friend that would design and teach you how to manage a website for free. You could answer questions during the slow times when you are not doing anything anyway. It would be a win-win situation.

In theory you are correct. A website could be a lucrative addition to your business.

It is possible to design website, register a domain name, and submit it to a website. But what happens next. Just like the physical shop the website will not do any business if there isn't any traffic. No one will visit your online store if they don't know about it.

The chances are good that your regular customers will probably check out your website, the ones that made items you have featured will probably tell their friends and families about it, but the chances are good that they won't buy anything, why should they pay for shipping and handling when they can drive a couple of miles and purchase it directly from you. Your tourist customers might buy from your online store but only if they know about it and since you probably waited until the slow season to create your website it will be months before you can tell them.

You could look into search engine optimization.

You might even want to consider something called pay-per-click.

Pay-per-click is a search engine that bases its rankings on something that is called a bid position. A website owner bids for an elevated position in the ranking when a certain keyword is typed into the search bar. The higher the bid, the higher the ranking.

Businesses that use pay-per-click prefer it to natural search engine optimization because it is an easy efficient way to improve a sites ranking and increase its traffic. Pay-per-click also lets webmaster maintain control over the search engine campaign.

People who forgo pay-per-click to natural search engine optimization say that the cost of pay-per-click is too high.

Chapter 22: 5 Ways to Improve your Search Engine Optimization at Minimal Cost

Search engine optimization (SEO) does not need to cost you anything. If you have time and patience, you can optimize your web site for search engines at minimal cost. This article outlines some of the key SEO ways you can use that do not cost you anything.

1. Write and submit a lot of articles. Articles are very powerful in building links to your website. All the articles you write are saved and archived in article directories, creating many links to your website. The more articles you write the better because as your articles are published by other websites, your website URL in the author's box will be on many websites. Writing articles need not cost you anything since you can write your own articles and then submit them to many article directories.

2. Create a web page on your website where you post your own articles. If you add new content on your website regularly, search engines will index your website, and your website ranking on these search engines will also increase. Make sure that you use your keywords and phrases in your web content as well as your articles.

3. Have your own blog and blog regularly using your keywords and phrases. You can simply sign up for own blog and start to blog right away. Have a link to

your website on your blog. Blogging and adding fresh content will make search engines crawl your blog. This process does not cost you anything. All you need is time to blog.

4. Have a link building strategy that will help you build many links to other related websites. This does not cost you anything. All you need to do is to contact webmasters you want to exchange links with. You can create one way links by articles submissions and forum participation among others.

5. Be patient and follow these SEO steps consistently. Your website will not rank high on search engines overnight. You will need to consistently work hard at writing articles, blogging and exchanging links so that you can see an increase in your website popularity rank. Patience is the most important trait you will need if you want to succeed in SEO for your website.

Follow these tips and increase your website popularity and rank on search engines. The easier your website is to find on search engines, the more traffic you get.

Chapter 23: Controversy Lends a Helping Hand to Search Engine Optimization

It is always wonderful to hear good news. Hearing good news makes us feel good about ourselves, the people around, our dog... heck the world is a better place when we have good news.

Good news might make us feel good about ourselves and the world but there is something deliciously appealing about bad news, especially if it is about someone other than ourselves.

Bad news makes good news copy. Celebrities know that. I once watched an interview with a well known, highly controversial, singer/songwriter, and performer. The newspapers are always full of articles and stories about his exploits. The interviewer asked this singer about one of his recent escapades. The singer kind of chuckled and shyly admitted that while the episode had happened it had been blown out of proportion. When the interviewer asked why the singer did nothing to correct the allegations the singer bluntly replied...money.

Each time someone accused him of doing something awful kids started to rush to the stores to buy his CD's, partly because his name was being splashed all over the airwaves and was fresh in their minds when the perused the music department, but also partly because their parents were trying to ban his music from the house. When he was on his best behaviour he did not get any media attention and his record sales plummeted. So, since the singer is anything but stupid and he has a deep appreciation for the things money can buy, he goes a little bit out of his way to perpetuate his bad boy image.

Bloggers are another group of people who understand how swiftly controversy spreads. They know that if they write about something that is controversial there will be a flood of readers reading their blogs and leaving feedback. Before you know it a dialogue has started, sometimes it isn't a peaceful dialogue but it is a dialogue just the same.

The same thing can be true about websites and search engine optimization. Search engine optimization is the art and science of making a web site appealing to search engines. Search engines determine the attractiveness of a website by sending out web crawlers that look for algorithms placed throughout the website. The more algorithms a website has the higher it gets ranked during a search.

A second thing several search engines look for is something called link analysis. Web crawlers look for how many links lead back to the website. The more links leading back to a website the higher that website will rank.

Controversy is a way to get a lot of links to your website fast. For example a breeder of Ball-headed pythons went to an exotic pet show to purchase some more snakes for his store. While he was at the show the police stormed the pet show, using excessive force to remove several of the exhibitors. You snapped several graphic pictures of the event, photos you later post on your website where you sell the snakes you breed. Others see the controversial photos posted on your site, they tell their friends and customers. To simplify things the owner of the second pet store posts a link on his site that attaches directly to yours. As more and more people hear about your photos, more and more links to your site are created. The next thing you know you are ranked on the very first page of the search engines hits.

In addition to the boost in your ranking you have also sold nearly all of your saleable snakes. Controversy really does sell.

Chapter 24: Google and Page Rank Search Engine Optimization's Dream Team

On September 7 1998, two Stanford University students, Larry Page and Sergey Brin, co-founded Google, a company they started as part of a research project in January 1996. On August 19, 2004 Google had its first public offering, the one point six-seven billion dollars it raised gave it a net worth of twenty-tree billion dollars. As of December 31, 2006 the Mountain View, California based internet search and online advertising company Google Inc. had over ten thousand full time employees. With a 50.8% market share, Google was the most used internet search engine at the end of 2006.

When Larry Page and Sergey Brin began creating Google it was based on the hypothesis that a search engine that could analyze the relationships between the different websites could get better results then the techniques that already existed. In the beginning the system used back links to estimate a websites importance causing its creators to name it Backrub.

Pleased with the results the search engine had on the Stanford University's website the two students registered the domain google.com on September 14, 1997. A year after registering the domain name Google Inc was incorporated.

Google began to sell advertisements associated with

keyword searches in 2000. By using text based advertisements Google was able to maintain an uncluttered page design that encouraged maximum page loading speed. Google sold the keywords based on a combination of click throughs and price bids. Bidding on the keywords started at five cents a click.

Google's simple design quickly attracted a large population of loyal internet users.

Google's success has allowed it the freedom to create tools and services such as Web applications, business solutions, and advertising networks for the general public and its expanding business environment.

In 2000 Google launched its advertising creation, AdWords. For a monthly fee Google would both set up and then manage a companies advertising campaign. Google relies on AdWords for the bulk of its revenue. AdWords offers its clients pay-per-click advertising. AdWords provides adverting for local, national, and international distribution. AdWords is able to define several important factors in keywords when and ad is first created to determine how much a client will pay-per-click, if the ad is eligible for ad auction, and how the ad ranks in the auction if it is eligible.

By following a set of guidelines provided by Google, webmasters can ensure that Google's web crawlers are able to find, index, and rank their websites.

Google offers a variety of webmaster tools that help provide information about add sites, updates, and sitemaps. Google's webmaster tools will provide statistics and error information about a site. The Google sitemaps will help webmasters know what mages are present on the website.

The major factor behind Google's success is its web search services. Google uses Page Rank for its search engine optimization program. Page rank is a link analysis algorithm that assigns a numerical weight to every single element of a hyperlinked set of documents, like the World Wide Web. Its purpose is to measure the relative importance within the set. PageRank is a registered trademark of Google. Stanford University owns PageRank's patent.

Chapter 25: Finding a Search Engine Optimization Company

When it comes to business some people like to get their hands dirty and iron out every little detail of every little deal and transaction. Others like to handle the parts of the business that they know and are comfortable with, leaving the bits and pieces they are unsure about to people who know what they are doing.

Before you start looking for a search engine optimization company sit down and consider your situation. What goals do you have for your website? What are your priorities? How much can you afford to spend, remember that you pay for quality, the lowest price is not always the best deal.

When it is time to submit your web-based business to a search engine there are search engine optimization companies who, for a fee, will be happy to optimize the websites for the business owners who do not feel comfortable doing it themselves.

Feel free to contact us via.
http://www.qualitywebdesign.aaglobalsourcing.com/contact-quality-web-desig if you would like coaching on SEO or help on how to use online marketing for your offline business or search engine optimize of your existing website. Your feedback is important to me.

The first thing you have to watch out for when you are selecting a company to handle your search engine optimization is scams. The first thing to do is avoid any search engine optimization companies that are listed in the black hat directory. Black hat search engine optimization is not really optimizing but really just spamdexing, most search engines penalize websites that are caught spamdexing. Also avoid any company who guarantees a ranking before they even look at your site. Make sure the company you are considering is actually going to do something besides add doorway pages and meta tags.

What is spamdexing?

Spamdexing is using methods that manipulate the relevancy or prominence of resources indexed by a search engine, usually in a manner that is inconsistent with the purpose of the indexing system. A lot of times spamdexing is done by stuffing a website full of keywords, web crawlers (the programs search engines use to rank websites) read the web sites they read lots of the same keyword and assume that the sight is content rich. Based on the web crawler's findings the website is given a high rank. A lot of the time the keywords are stuck at the bottom of the document where the internet user can't see them. Keyword stuffing is considered content spam.

The other common type of spamdexing is link spam. Link spam is spamdexing that takes advantage of link ranking algorithms causing search engines to give the guilty website a higher ranking. Link farms, hidden links, Sybil attack, wiki spam, spam blogs (also referred to as splogs), page hijacking, buying expired domains, and referrer log spamming are forms of link spam.

Chapter 26: Search Engine Optimization: Art and Science

One of the basic components of the Internet is the search engine. A search engine, as its name implies, helps people look for pertinent websites and web pages which contain information based on the keywords that the surfers have encoded. A survey revealed that around 90% of Internet users utilize search engines in doing their Internet-related activities.

Websites are developed for the main reason of being viewed. They are portals which provide information that are intended to reach their target audience. This is the main context which explains the importance of search engines.

Being listed in search engines is one thing and being listed on the top lists of the search engines is another thing. When someone searches for a certain keyword through the search engine, the most popular websites appear first and are usually the most visited websites. There are factors that search engines consider when they rank websites according to keywords. This is the main task of search engine optimization (SEO).

SEO?

Search engine optimization consists of methods which aim at improving a website's ranking in search engines" listings. SEO has become one of the sunshine industries that are related to the Internet. There are multiple ways on how to do search engine optimization and many companies have dealt into this business.

How do Search Engines Operate?

To be able to appreciate the beauty of the art and science of search engine optimization, one must be able to understand how search engines work. One may not be able to fully grasp the nitty-gritty details of search engine optimization operations, but he can appreciate it to a level that he realizes the importance that it plays in effectively marketing his website.

Search engines rank websites in different ways. A website can primarily be listed by a search engine as a sponsored link or a pay-per-click advertisement or as a result of organic search.

With the continuous development of search engines, many search engines have introduced paid advertising. Website owners can actually bid to be displayed on top of the website listings of search engines. The most popular example of this system is the Google Adwords system, which is displayed at the right-hand side corner of the browser when one uses the Google search engine.

A website can also be listed through organic search. Search engines use 'spiders" and "robots" to be able to assess the contents of a website and they then relay the information to the main search engine system so that when a surfer searches for a certain topic, the websites which are organized to contain that topic appear first. Search engine optimization is aimed primarily to be able to do certain things to a website so as to achieve optimal organization to reflect a certain keyword or topic.

History of SEO

Search engine optimization can be traced back to the mid-1900s. During those times, the search engines initiated the cataloguing of the contents of the Internet. Webmasters needed to submit their websites to different search engines to be able to get the attention of the engines" spiders. The spiders collected, collated and reported the information to the search engines. The engines would then arrange the websites according to topic and displayed the websites when the keyword or topic is searched by surfers.

Meta tags were used by webmasters to be recognized by the search engines. Then, abuse of meta tags became rampant, causing websites to dominate searches that are irrelevant to them. Search engines began to fight back by using more complex algorithms which took into consideration other factors such as the text that is contained within the tile, the domain name, the file names, the keyword density, the keyword proximity, and other such factors.

Today

Today, the newly developed websites do not need to

submit to the search engines to be noticed. Spiders today are capable of tracking down websites even through links that are in the website. The use of a site map or hypertext links can help the spiders to navigate the site.

The industry of search engine optimization is a booming one. As the Internet takes people's lives into more advanced stages, it has become more and more important terms of information dissemination, business development and communications. Having one's website noticed by search engines is a good way to start the whole Internet journey.

Chapter 27: How Title and Meta Tags are used for Search Engine Optimization

When it comes to title tags and search engine optimization there are a few question website owners typically ask. Does each individual web page need a different title? Is there a maximum length for title tags? Is there a title tag limit? Are title Meta tags a good idea?

The World Wide Web Consortium requires that every single HTML document must have a title element in the head section. They also state that the title element should be used to identify each individual pages content.

The title tag plays four separate roles on the internet.

The first role the title tag fulfills is what librarians, other webmasters, and directory editors use to link to other websites. A well written title tag is far more likely to get faster reviews than one that is sloppy or incomprehendable.

The title tag is what is displayed on the visitor's browser. By displaying the title tag in the visitors browser the web user knows exactly where they are if they have to return to the site later on. Internet Explorer typically tires to display the first ninety-five characters of the title tag.

Search engines display the title tag as the most important piece of information available to web searchers.

A good title tag should be able to clearly indicate the webpage's contents to the web user. A clear title tag is more likely to be placed in the user's favorites list. The normal length for a good clear title tag is normally under sixty-five characters long. Title tags should be typed in the title case. Headers should also be typed in the title case.

When it comes to search engine optimization, the home page title is normally the first thing the web crawlers look at when they are ranking a webpage. Your website is introduced by your homepage title. It is important to make sure that your title tag sounds credible.

Every single page of your website must have its very own unique title. A Meta tag is a special HTML tag that provides information about a web page. Meta tags do not affect the display of a webpage. Although Meta tags are placed directly into the HTML code, they are invisible to web users. Search engines use Meta tags to help correctly categorize a page. Meta tags are a critical part of search engine optimization.

It is important to remember that Meta tags are not a magic solution to making your website a raging success. The most valuable feature Meta tags offer to website owners is the ability to control (to a certain degree) how their web pages are described by the search engines. Meta tags can also let website owners prevent having their website indexed at all.

Meta tag keywords are a way to provide extra test for web crawler based search engines to index. While this is great in theory several of the major search engines have crawlers that ignore the HTML and focus entirely on the body of the webpage.

Chapter 28: Newer is not Always Better when it Involves Search Engine Optimization

We live in a world where everybody wants the latest and greatest, somewhere along the way we have come to the conclusion that the newer something is the better. If we are buying a CD it has to be the latest release from the new one hit wonder, we don't care if the song writer could not tell melody from harmony or that the singer is incapable of carrying a tune, all that matters is that it is new.

Each time new car registration is due to come out hundreds of people scramble to get to car dealerships, frantic to drive the new registration cars, barely capable of waiting for them to be unloaded off the truck, it does not matter if we are six months behind on car payments on last years model which is in perfect running condition, we are blinded by all the bells and whistles that the new cars have to offer. People will stand in a long line, overnight, in an electrical storm to simply to spend an unhealthy amount of money on the latest electronic gadget just because it is brand new, we do not care that in just a few months it will be a fraction of the cost, we have to have it now.

Even internet service suffers from the right now syndrome. For years we were content with dialup service. Sure it was slow but it was that or nothing. Heck we hardly noticed that it took hours to download a simple, days to upload a couple of pictures, download a video... that was practically unheard off. We did not know any better. Now that the world has found out about all the new options for internet service we have to have that. It does not matter that it is double the monthly cost or we have to default on are student loans in order to purchase the necessary equipment. If it is cordless, faster, and designed with the latest technology we have to have it...right now.

We do not care if the old stuff is made with better materials, last longer, and is cheaper. In our minds old equals junk.

Search engine optimization is one spot where we should force ourselves to shed our weird inhibitions about old stuff. When it comes to search engine optimization, age rules over youth.

Search engine optimization is the art and science of making web pages attractive to the search engines. The more attractive a web site appears (search engines are attracted, not to beauty, but to repetitious algorithms) the higher it ranks in the search engines search result. A low ranking could potentially be the kiss of death to an internet based business because studies have shown the internet users seldom look past the second page of hits.

Search engines use web crawlers to determine a websites ranking.

Older websites and the webmasters who manage

them have had more time to develop and maintain their algorithms. They are already itemized and ranked by the search engines, in some cases it can take three months for a web crawler to get around to spidering a brand new website that has been submitted to the search engine, old sites are already appearing and gaining customer recognition. If an older site has been around long enough to have earned a loyal customer base, even if a shuffle in the rankings causes the aged web site to be bumped from prime ranking position, loyal customers will still look for it.

Chapter 29: Search Engine Marketing-how it Differs from Search Engine Optimization

Search engine marketing is a set of marketing methods used to increase the visibility of a website in search engine results pages. Types of search engine marketing include; search engine optimization, pay per click, paid inclusion, and social media optimization. Search engine marketing differs from search engine optimization which is the art and science of making web pages attractive to internet search engines.

Non-profit organizations, universities, political parties, and the government can all benefit from search engine marketing. Businesses that sell products and/or services online can use search engine marketing to help improve their sales figures.

Some of the goals of search engine marketing are to develop a brand, generate media coverage, and enhancing a reputation, and to drive business to a physical location.

If you do not feel confident enough to try your own search engine marketing there are several companies that will be able to help you out for a price. If you decide to go with a search engine marketing company take your time and shop around, find a company that really suits your own businesses search engine marketing needs.

Stay away from companies that promise top rankings. Most companies that promise top ranking are more interested in your money than they are in keeping your business. Quite often this type of company will charge you top money, spend a few days making sure your website has a few basic requirements and that is the last you hear from them. This type of search engine marketing company is not really interested in repeat customers.

Tread carefully around companies that promise first page rankings on the major search engines like Google and Yahoo. Make sure these companies are talking about sponsored listings and not just natural listings. Companies that are only after natural listings traditionally charge a large monthly fee, using a small portion of the money on sponsored listings, and pocketing the remainder.

The false promise most commonly used by shady search engine marketing companies is the money back guarantee. Generally if you read the contract very carefully you will lean that these companies have a very strange idea of major search engine. Companies that have a money back guarantee typically do not deal with the search engine movers and shakers like Google and Yahoo, instead they use small obscure search engines that are hardly ever used.

Feel free to contact us via. http://www.qualitywebdesign.aaglobalsourcing.com/contact-quality-web-desig if you would like coaching on SEO or help on how to use online marketing for your offline business or search engine optimize of your existing website. Your feedback is important to me.

We are created to offer the public educational resources about search engine marketing and to also promote search engine marketing. Currently we represents over 50 global search engine marketing companies. We are happy to offer our resources to the public for a small fee. We also offer search engine marketing training courses for any and all interested parties who would like to expand their knowledge of search engine marketing. Our objectives are to teach search engine marketing strategies, techniques, and successful practices, to increase the availability and quality of its professionals, and to offer training courses that will help to establish a benchmark for search engine marketing. The cost of our training course can range anywhere from five hundred pounds for a fundamentals of search marketing class, to over two thousand pounds for an advanced search advertising course.

Chapter 30: How Google's Pagerank Determines Search Engine Optimization

Some internet search engines are set up to look for keywords throughout a webpage, they then use a mathematical equation that takes in the amount of time the keywords appears on the webpage and factors it with the location of the keywords to determine the ranking of the webpage.

Other internet search engines use a process that judges the amount of times a webpage is linked to other web pages to determine how a webpage is ranked. The process of using links to determine search engine ranking is called link analysis.

Keyword searches and link analysis are both part of a routine internet search engine procedure called search engine optimization. Search engine optimization is the art and science of making a website attractive to search engines, the more attractive a website appears to the search engine the higher it will rank in searches and in the world of internet searches ranking is everything.

As 2006 faced its last weeks, Google was the internet search engine that most internet users preferred. Approximately fifty percent of the times a consumer turned to a search engine for their internet needs they turned to Google. Yahoo! was the second favourite.

Most of Google's popularity is credited to its preferred form of search engine optimization, a trademarked program Google dubbed PageRank. When PageRank was patented the patent was assigned to Stanford University.

PageRank was designed by Larry Page, (the name is a play on his name) and Sergey Brin while they were students at Stanford University as part of a research project they were working on about internet search engines.

PageRank is based on the link analyses algorithm. PageRank is described as a link analysis algorithm that assigns a numerical weight to each individual element of a hyperlink set of documents. The purpose is to measure its relative important with the set. The numerical weight assigned to any element is called PageRank of E. PR(E) is the denotation used.

PageRank operates on a system similar to a voting booth. Each time it finds a hyperlink to a webpage, PageRank counts that hyperlink as a vote that supports the webpage. The more pages that link to the page, the more votes of support the webpage receives. If PageRank comes across a website that has absolutely no links connecting it to another webpage then it is not awarded any votes at all.

Tests done with a model like PageRank have shown that the system is not infallible.

The HITS algorithm is an alternate to the PageRank algorithm.

Google's powers that be take a dim view on spamdexing. In 2005 Google designed and activated a program called nofollow, a program they designed to allow webmasters and bloggers to create links that PageRank would ingnore. The same system was also used to keep spamdexing to a minumum.

Google has designed PageRank to be an eight-unit measurement. Google displays the value PageRank places on each website directly beside each website it displays.

It has been proposed that a version of PageRank should be used to replace ISI impact factor so that the quality of a journal citation can be determined.

Chapter 31: Marketing Online with Organic Search Engine Optimization

Basically, marketing is about helping customers/ prospects find your website/business - looking to grow your business, increase sales leads, or lower customer acquisition costs. You have already read about one way to do that, but smart marketing means you will use a combination of both SEO AND PPC. Call it online search engine advertising if you will - it works and generates new business.

To be even more specific: organic search engine optimization is the process of optimizing a web site or page so it ranks well in the free listings of the search engines. This is the best (and least expensive) option for getting visitors. Why? Visitors click on free organic listings more often than paid listings. Something else you need to know so you realize just how important this is for your site. Just about 65% of business websites were created solely for customers without any search engine optimization.

Translation: two thirds of businesses on the web are in the bottom of engine results. Since approximately 85% of online sales come from search engine traffic – you have got a problem. Without getting into too much detail about "how-to" accomplish this organic optimization - suffice it to say the methods are called "White Hat" and involve keyword research, key phrase placement in your Meta tags and content, and the application of special formatting such as headers, bold and bullets. Remember to do both online AND offline optimization. This includes regularly submitting to directories, writing press releases, submitting articles, and getting other links pointing back to your site.

To get relevant links - start a blog about your key phrase. Link from it to your web site, and keep the content on both fresh and original. The good news? 70% of search engine users visit organic sites, and 50% of them select the top results. Imagine what that will mean for your marketing site.

Google AdWords offers you:

Targeted reach: Now you can advertise to people searching on Google. Even if you already appear in Google's search results, AdWords can help you target new audiences on Google and our advertising network.

Greater control: You can edit your ads and adjust your budget until you get the results you want. You can also display a variety of ad formats and even target your ads to specific languages and geographic locations.

Measurable value: There is no minimum spending requirement or time commitment. And with the cost-per-click option, you are only charged if people click your ads. This means every dollar of your budget goes toward bringing new prospects to you.

Local and regional targeting: Set your ads to appear only to people searching in a particular region. Now it is easy to target online customers within, say, 25 miles of your front door. Learn more Local business ads. Get noticed on Google Maps. People searching for information related to your business will see your location, contact information, and an image of your choosing highlighted on a map of your area.

Chapter 32: Conclusion

Search engine optimization is the process of making sure that your website content and information helps you to achieve high ranking on search engines such that you will get traffic directed to your website through these search engines.

The very first and important step in search engine optimization (SEO) is to know all your niche keywords and phrases, and this begins with a good knowledge of your niche. If you want to attract some potential customers to your website, you should know the relevant keywords and phrases to use. When people are looking for information online, they type different keywords and phrases on search engines, and you will need to know these keywords and phrases. By having these keywords in your website content, your website will show up on search engines when people look for information that relates to these keywords.

Make maximum use of your keywords and key phrases. In order to make sure that your website is found by search engines, you will need to have your keywords in your web content and on your blog. Make sure that your web content is keyword rich. Use your keywords in all the articles that you write.

Build your website such that your keywords and phrases are included in the content of your website, including the headlines on your website.

Expand one way and two way links to your website. Link building is one of the most effective ways to increase the visibility of your website on search engines. Build one way links by submitting articles with your website URL in the resources box, and participate in relevant forums and have your URL in your signature. Write product reviews and post them at other related websites and include your website URL. You can also exchange two way links with other web masters for related web sites. The more websites you have linking back to your website, the better your web site ranking will be on search engines.

Submit your website to website directories. This will help to improve your page ranking on search engines and will also drive traffic to your website. SEO is very important for the success of your website. Follow the steps outlined above and make your website visible on search engines. If your website ranking is high on search engines, it means that you can be easily found and a lot of traffic will be driven to your website.

Good Luck!